What do you know about ?

PLANTS
and
ANIMALS

Over 101 Questions and ANSWERS

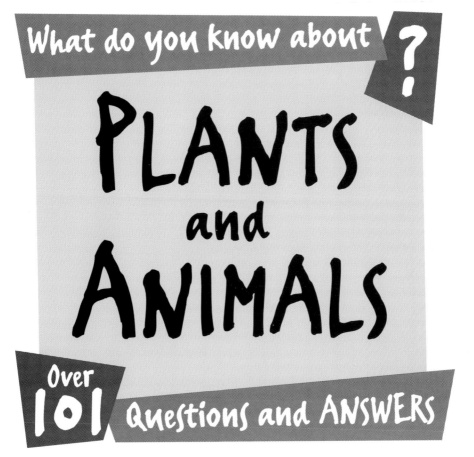

Written by
Andrew Langley & Paul Sterry

Vineyard BOOKS

Planned and produced by
Andromeda Oxford Limited
11-15 The Vineyard
Abingdon
Oxon OX14 3PX

Copyright © Andromeda Oxford Limited 1998

ISBN 1 86199 029 4

Printed in Singapore

CONTENTS

HABITATS

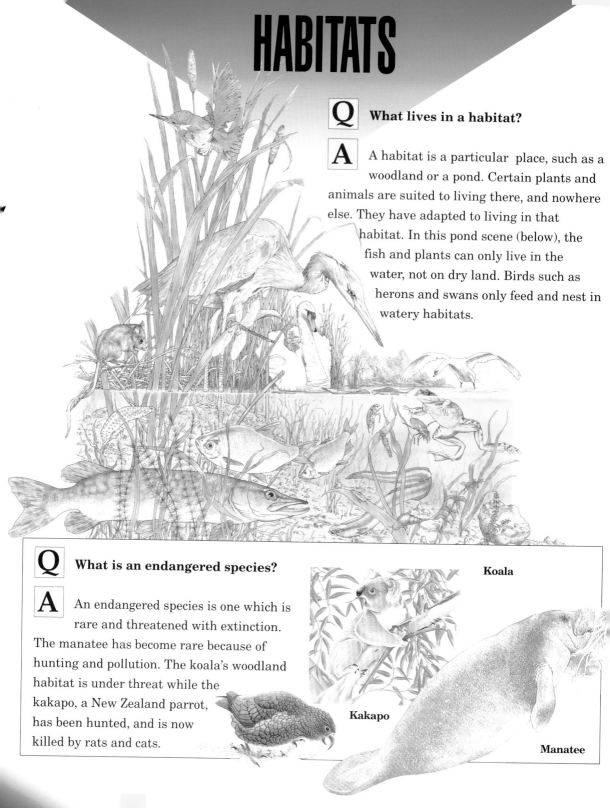

Q What lives in a habitat?

A A habitat is a particular place, such as a woodland or a pond. Certain plants and animals are suited to living there, and nowhere else. They have adapted to living in that habitat. In this pond scene (below), the fish and plants can only live in the water, not on dry land. Birds such as herons and swans only feed and nest in watery habitats.

Q What is an endangered species?

A An endangered species is one which is rare and threatened with extinction. The manatee has become rare because of hunting and pollution. The koala's woodland habitat is under threat while the kakapo, a New Zealand parrot, has been hunted, and is now killed by rats and cats.

Koala

Kakapo

Manatee

Q **How do habitats change?**

A Although people alter habitats, the process also happens naturally. This cross-section through a pond (right) shows the gradual process of filling-in. Over the years, the roots of the water plants trap silt, so the pond holds less and less water. The pond becomes silted up and will eventually become dry land.

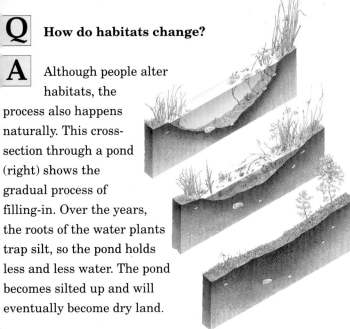

Q **What is a food web?**

A A food web (below) is a way of showing how plants and animals in a habitat depend on each other. The arrows show which species provide food for other species. Some of the small animals are food for a number of larger predators.

Q **How do animals adapt to changes in their environment?**

A In many parts of the world the environment changes with the seasons. When winter comes, some animals hibernate while others migrate. The arctic hare has adapted to winter snowfall by moulting its brown summer coat for a white winter one. This gives it camouflage throughout the year.

Q **What is a microhabitat?**

A Every habitat contains lots of smaller habitats called microhabitats. The creatures that live there are specially adapted to its conditions. These mites, for example, can only survive among particles of soil.

PLANT KINGDOM

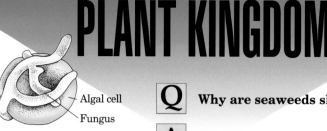

Algal cell

Fungus

Q What are lichens?

A Lichens (above) are curious plants. They are made up of algal cells, surrounded by a fungus. The same alga can live alone but the fungus needs the alga to survive, because the alga can make food from sunlight energy. Lichens live on stones and trees and grow slowly.

Q Why are seaweeds slimy?

A Seaweeds (right) are simple plants that grow on the seashore. There are lots of different types but most feel slimy to the touch. This is because there is a thin, jelly-like layer on the seaweed surface. The jelly-like layer prevents the seaweed from being damaged by the waves.

Q What are fungi?

A Fungi belong to a group of organisms separate from plants and animals. Unlike plants, they have no green pigment and cannot make their own food. The main part of a large fungus is a huge network of tiny threads in the ground. These take up food from the soil or from dead plants and animals. At certain times of year, spore-producing mushrooms and toadstools like those shown here emerge.

Fly agaric

Blusher

Bracket fungus

Cage fungus

Earthball

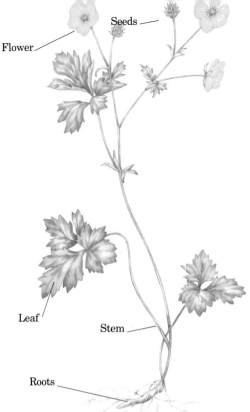

Seeds

Flower

Leaf

Stem

Roots

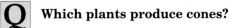

Q Which plants produce cones?

A Plants that produce cones are called conifers (below). Conifers often grow as large trees which are themselves cone-shaped in outline. Cones are the parts of the conifer used for reproduction, so there are male and female cones. Male cones produce pollen which is carried by the wind to fertilise the female cone. This then develops and matures. Seeds form between the hard, protective scales of the cone and are released when ripe.

Pine cone

Fir cone

Conifer tree

Q What are the parts of a flowering plant called?

A A flowering plant (above) usually has roots anchoring it in the soil. These take up water and nutrients. Above ground, a stem carries these to the leaves. The leaves use sunlight energy to make food. At the ends of the stem are flowers, the reproductive parts. Once fertilised, the flowers produce seeds.

Q How is timber cut from a tree trunk?

A A felled tree trunk is first stripped of its branches. It is then cut lengthways in an ordered way so that no timber is wasted. First, two sides of the trunk are cut to produce thin planks of wood. Then the central part of the tree trunk is cut into thicker lengths of wood suitable for building work.

PLANT LIFE

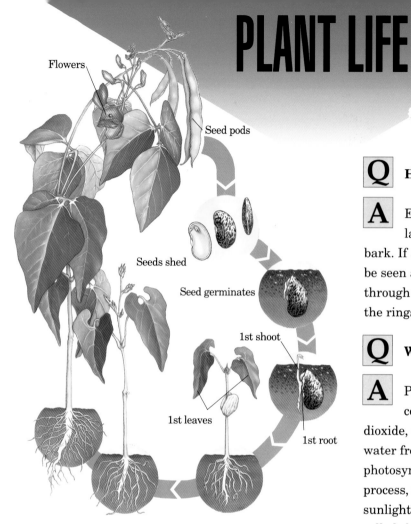

Flowers

Seed pods

Seeds shed

Seed germinates

1st shoot

1st leaves

1st root

 Q How can you tell a tree's age?

A Every year a tree grows a new layer of wood just beneath the bark. If a tree is cut down, the layers can be seen as rings in the cross-section through the stump (above). By counting the rings you can tell its age.

Q Why do plants need sunlight?

A Plants make their own food by combining a gas called carbon dioxide, which they get from the air, with water from the soil. This process is called photosynthesis (below). To power the process, the plant uses the energy of sunlight. A green pigment in the leaves called chlorophyll traps the Sun's energy.

 Q How does a plant complete its life cycle?

A Every year, plants (above) produce large numbers of seeds which fall to the ground. Many die but some will germinate. Tiny roots and shoots grow from the seed and soon the plant increases in size. As the plant grows larger, more and more leaves are produced and eventually flowers appear. Pollen from male flowers fertilises female flowers and the base of the flower begins to swell. It is here that this year's seeds are being made, completing the plant's life cycle.

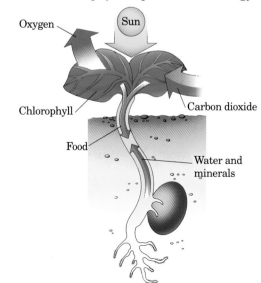

Oxygen

Sun

Chlorophyll

Carbon dioxide

Food

Water and minerals

Q Which plants eat animals?

A Venus fly traps and pitcher plants
(right) can absorb nutrients from
animals. Venus fly traps have leaves which
trap insects and digest them. Pitcher plants
have flask-shaped leaves in which water
collects. Insects fall in and drown.

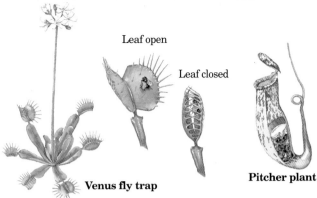

Leaf open

Leaf closed

Pitcher plant

Venus fly trap

Q What are fruit 'pips'?

A Fruit pips are the seeds of the
plant which produced the fruit.
There are many types of fruit but most
are juicy and nutritious, which make
animals eat them. The seed may be swallowed whole and
passed out in the animal's droppings later on. In this way,
the plant has its seeds scattered, or dispersed.

Q Why do plants produce flowers?

A Plants produce flowers (below) to reproduce and
create a new generation. Flowers bear the male
and female parts. Many flowers
have colours and scents which
attract insects. The insects
take male pollen to the
female parts of other
flowers. The pollen of
some flowers is
carried by the wind.

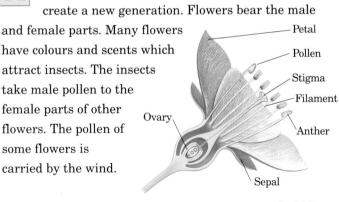

Petal

Pollen

Stigma

Filament

Ovary

Anther

Sepal

Orchid

Fritillaria

Clematis

Silver birch

Q How do daffodils survive the winter?

A Daffodils have leaves and
flowers above ground only
for a few months each
spring. During the winter
they live as onion-
shaped bulbs buried
in the ground. Bulbs are
protected from
winter frosts
by the soil
above them.

Bulb cross-section

PREHISTORIC LIFE

Q What were the first animals like?

A The first animals were probably single-celled creatures. Their bodies had no hard parts so they did not form fossils. The first animals that we know from fossils lived 570 million years ago. Many had worm-like or plant-like bodies. Others had armoured head shields (below).

Q How did *Pterodactylus* fly?

A *Pterodactylus* (above) had a lightweight, furry body and was able to fly using its long, membranous wings. These were attached to the wrist bones and the bones of the fourth finger. *Pterodactylus* probably clung to cliff edges and then launched itself into the air, where it glided over the sea snatching fish from the surface.

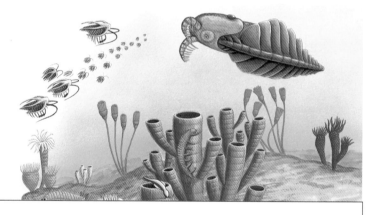

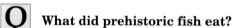

Q What did prehistoric fish eat?

A Although no-one can be completely sure, the diet of prehistoric fish probably consisted of worm-like creatures and molluscs. Some of the larger species of fish had numerous sharp teeth. They might have chased and eaten other fish, in a similar way to modern-day sharks and barracudas.

Ichthyosaurus

Cryptoclidus

Peloneustes

Q Which reptiles ruled the seas?

A In ancient times, the seas were ruled by ichthyosaurs and plesiosaurs (above). Both had streamlined bodies and paddle-shaped limbs. *Ichthyosaurus* resembled a cross between a fish and a dolphin. Some plesiosaurs, such as *Cryptoclidus,* had long necks; others, like *Peloneustes*, were whale-like. Ichthyosaurs and plesiosaurs ate mainly fish, but some plesiosaurs also ate one another.

Q How did mammals survive the Ice Age?

A As the Ice Age approached and the climate became colder, many mammals grew larger. This is because large animals retain their body heat better than small ones. Heat retention was also helped by growing thick, furry coats, such as that seen in the woolly mammoth (left). Thick layers of fat beneath the skin provided insulation. Other large, hairy mammals that survived the Ice Age included woolly rhinoceroses and giant cave bears.

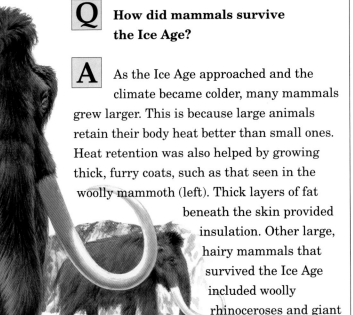

Q What were the terror cranes?

A Terror cranes were giant birds that lived some 50 million years ago in North America. They stood 2 metres tall and hunted small mammals in areas of open grassland. They had strong legs for running and a powerful, hook-tipped bill for dealing with their prey. Terror cranes are given the scientific name *Diatryma.*

DINOSAURS

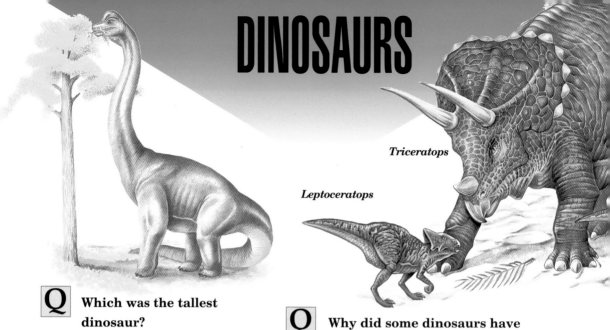

Triceratops

Leptoceratops

Q Which was the tallest dinosaur?

A Many of the huge, plant-eating dinosaurs had long necks. The tallest was *Brachiosaurus* (above) which not only had a long neck but long front legs as well. It could stretch up to 12 metres and probably fed on the tops of trees, much as giraffes do today. It needed legs the size of tree trunks to support its great weight.

Q Why did some dinosaurs have armoured heads?

A Some dinosaurs were meat-eating predators. Not surprisingly, many of the plant-eating dinosaurs developed armoured heads to help defend themselves (above). The head of *Triceratops* was covered with a large plate and carried three, forward-pointing horns. *Leptoceratops* was much smaller and lacked *Triceratops*' horns.

Q Which was the most fearsome meat-eater?

A *Tyrannosaurus* (right) was probably the most terrifying carnivorous dinosaur. It was certainly one of the largest. The head was huge and its skull was larger than a man. *Tyrannosaurus* stood upright on massive hind legs and could outrun slower, plant-eating dinosaurs. Its teeth, which were 15 centimetres long, were used to rip and tear the flesh of its prey.

Tyrannosaurus skull

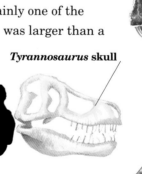

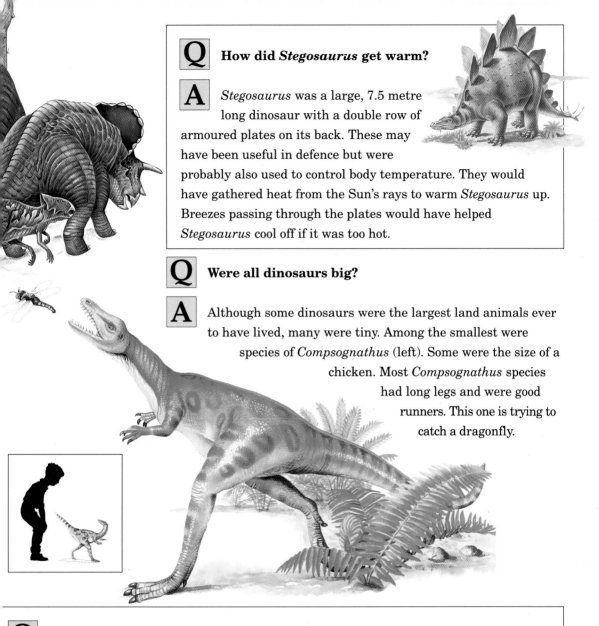

Q How did *Stegosaurus* get warm?

A *Stegosaurus* was a large, 7.5 metre long dinosaur with a double row of armoured plates on its back. These may have been useful in defence but were probably also used to control body temperature. They would have gathered heat from the Sun's rays to warm *Stegosaurus* up. Breezes passing through the plates would have helped *Stegosaurus* cool off if it was too hot.

Q Were all dinosaurs big?

A Although some dinosaurs were the largest land animals ever to have lived, many were tiny. Among the smallest were species of *Compsognathus* (left). Some were the size of a chicken. Most *Compsognathus* species had long legs and were good runners. This one is trying to catch a dragonfly.

Q How do we know what dinosaurs looked like?

A We can tell what dinosaurs looked like from fossils. These are found in sedimentary rocks from all over the world. Often just a few dinosaur bones are found but sometimes scientists discover a complete skeleton.

SIMPLE CREATURES

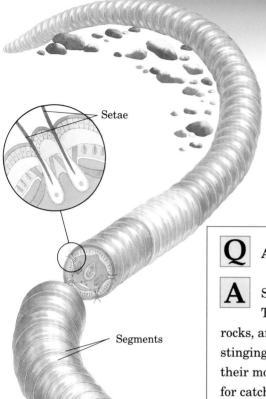

Setae

Segments

Mouth

Q What is inside an earthworm?

A An earthworm's body (left) is made up of compartments called segments. The intestine and the nervous system run the entire length of the body. The hearts, brain and reproductive organs are found near the front of the body. Each segment carries bristly hairs called setae. These help the worm grip the ground when moving.

Q Are sea anemones plants or animals?

A Sea anemones are simple marine animals. They live attached to rocks, and have a ring of stinging tentacles around their mouth which they use for catching food. Some sea anemones can pull the tentacles inside (right).

Q What is a protozoan?

A Protozoans are tiny animals made from a single cell. Although small, these cells are very complex and enable the animal to feed, breathe, excrete and reproduce. Protozoans are very common in soil and water. Some have a rigid shape while others have no fixed shape at all.

Actinosphaerium

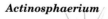

Volvox

Amoeba

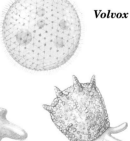

Difflugia

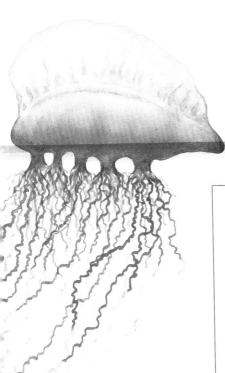

Q How does a Portuguese Man o' War swim?

A The Portuguese Man o' War (left) is a large, poisonous, jellyfish-like creature with tentacles up to 18 metres long. It lives in the ocean but does not actually swim. It has a float filled with air which keeps it on the surface, and a sail which carries the animal on the breeze.

Q Why do crabs walk sideways?

A Crabs have their walking legs placed beneath their bodies. If it were to walk forwards or backwards, the crab would trip over its own legs. Instead, crabs scuttle sideways over the seabed so their legs do not touch.

Q How does the cleaner shrimp get its name?

 The cleaner shrimp (below) removes parasites from fish such as this butterfly fish. Both animals benefit. The shrimp gets a tasty meal and the fish loses a parasite which it would be unable to dislodge on its own.

Q What simple animal is destroying the Great Barrier Reef?

 The crown of thorns starfish (below) lives in tropical seas. It is common on the Great Barrier Reef off the coast of Australia. It turns its stomach inside out to eat the soft-bodied coral animals. Its skin is armoured with fearsome spines and it has few predators. The crown of thorns has destroyed large areas of coral reef.

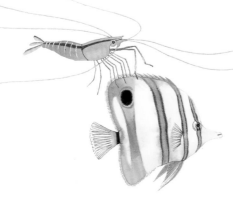

INSECTS & SPIDERS

Q How does a spider make a web?

A Spiders make silk in glands near their abdomens. They draw the silk out into threads to build insect traps called webs. The orb spider (right) first fixes threads in a box shape. Then it weaves more threads to the centre. The threads are covered in sticky droplets to catch insects.

Q What is a stick insect?

A Stick insects (right) have long thin bodies with brown or green colouring which makes them look just like the twigs or leaves they sit on. Their enemies, such as birds or lizards, often fail to see them. If they are attacked, stick insects fall to the ground and lie still, once again becoming difficult to see.

Q What is inside an insect?

A An insect's body (right) has many of the organs we have, such as a brain and a heart, but they work differently. Insects breathe through holes called spiracles in their hard outer covering. Their gut is a tube running from the mouth to the end of the abdomen. Their blood runs in an open system throughout the body. All the organs are bathed in blood.

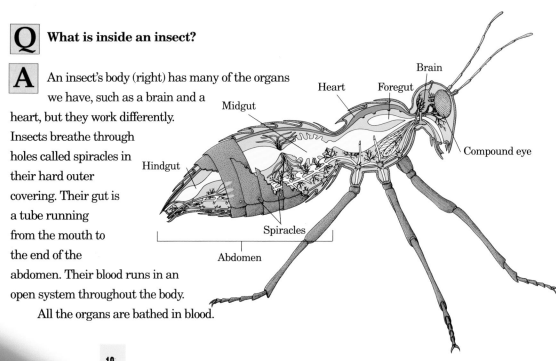

Brain

Heart

Foregut

Midgut

Compound eye

Hindgut

Spiracles

Abdomen

Q **Which is the heaviest insect?**

A The African Goliath beetle (left) is the heaviest of all insects. It grows as long as 12 cm and weighs up to 110 grams. The lightest insect is the parasitic wasp, the fairy fly, which is less than 0.2 mm long and weighs just 0.006 grams.

Q **What do bees and wasps eat?**

Bee   Wasp

A Bees eat pollen and nectar which they collect from plants and store in their nests, and turn into honey. Wasps kill other insects as food for their young, or larvae.

Q **How do grasshoppers 'sing'?**

A Grasshoppers make sounds by rubbing small pegs on their hind legs against a hard vein on their forewings. Males 'sing' to attract a mate.

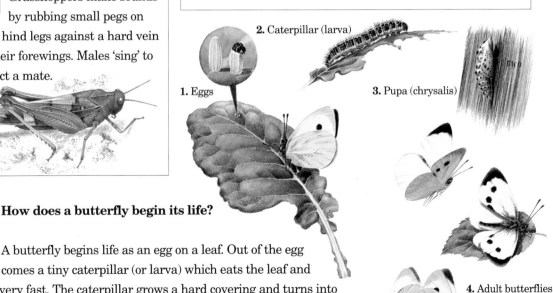

1. Eggs

2. Caterpillar (larva)

3. Pupa (chrysalis)

4. Adult butterflies

Q **How does a butterfly begin its life?**

A A butterfly begins life as an egg on a leaf. Out of the egg comes a tiny caterpillar (or larva) which eats the leaf and grows very fast. The caterpillar grows a hard covering and turns into a pupa (or chrysalis). After several days, or even weeks, the pupa case splits open and the butterfly crawls out. As soon as its wings have dried, it can fly away (right).

FISH

Q Which fish climbs trees?

A The mudskipper (below) lives in African mangrove swamps. Because it can take in oxygen through its mouth and throat, it can venture on to the mudflats when the tide is out. If danger threatens and it cannot get back to its burrow, it can climb mangrove roots to escape.

Q What is unusual about the seahorse?

A Apart from its curious shape, the seahorse (right) is unusual because it is the male and not the female which looks after the eggs and young. He has a brood pouch on his belly and this can hold up to 200 eggs and young. When the young are old enough, the male expels them from the pouch.

Q How does a fish sense its surroundings?

A Although most fish have good eyesight and a sense of taste, they also use a structure called the lateral line (right). This groove lies along the side of a fish's body, and contains special cells that are sensitive to vibrations in the water. With this, the fish can detect both food and danger.

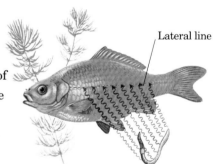

Lateral line

Q How does a shark hunt its prey?

A Although sharks have poor eyesight, they have an excellent sense of smell. They can detect blood diluted a million times in water and will home-in on a wounded animal in the sea. Sharks are also able to detect vibrations in the water caused, for example, by the thrashing movements of an injured fish.

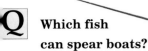

Q Which fish can spear boats?

A Although they do not do it often, swordfish (right) have been known to spear the hulls of wooden boats. They have a snout which is long and pointed. It carries rows of small, sharp teeth along the sides, rather like the blade of a saw. The swordfish probably uses this to slash at prey and predators.

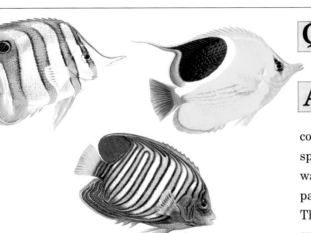

Q How do butterfly fish get their name?

A Butterfly fish get their name because they are very brightly coloured, like the wings of a butterfly. Most species are found on coral reefs in tropical waters around the world. The colours and patterns are thought to confuse predators. They may also help the fish blend into its surroundings to hide from predators.

Q How does a flounder avoid its enemies?

A The flounder (below) is a flatfish that lives on the sandy seabed. Its markings and colours help it blend in with its surroundings, for camouflage. The flounder can also flick sand over its body using its fins. Often only the head and eyes remain visible.

FISH

Q What are the main parts of a fish?

A The main parts on the outside of a fish are the gills (for breathing), the fins (for swimming and steering) and the lateral line (for detecting movement nearby).

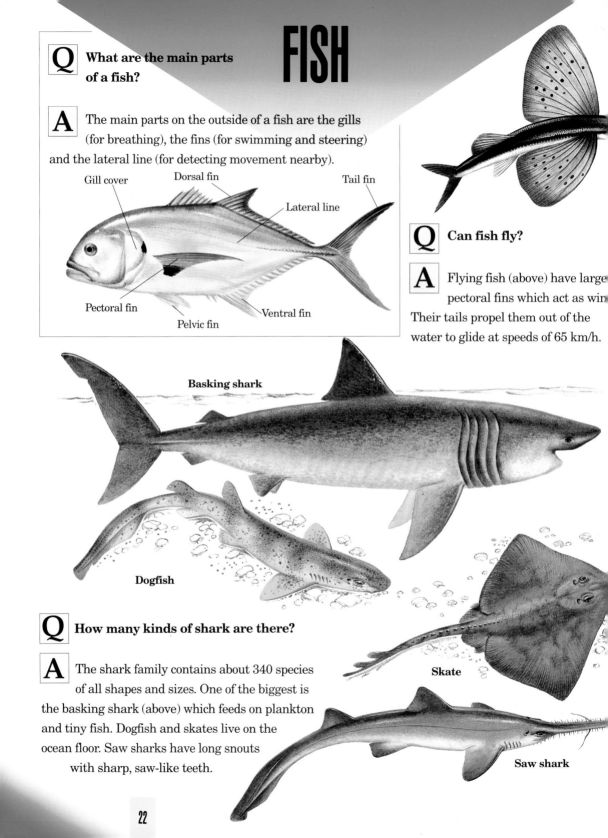

Gill cover

Dorsal fin

Tail fin

Lateral line

Pectoral fin

Ventral fin

Pelvic fin

Q Can fish fly?

A Flying fish (above) have large pectoral fins which act as wings. Their tails propel them out of the water to glide at speeds of 65 km/h.

Basking shark

Dogfish

Skate

Saw shark

Q How many kinds of shark are there?

A The shark family contains about 340 species of all shapes and sizes. One of the biggest is the basking shark (above) which feeds on plankton and tiny fish. Dogfish and skates live on the ocean floor. Saw sharks have long snouts with sharp, saw-like teeth.

Q Which fish swims the fastest?

A Sailfish are the fastest swimmers, reaching speeds of up to 109 km/h. The fish's large dorsal fin can lie flat against its body when it is swimming at speed to help streamline it.

Loosejaw

Viperfish

Anglerfish

Hatchetfish

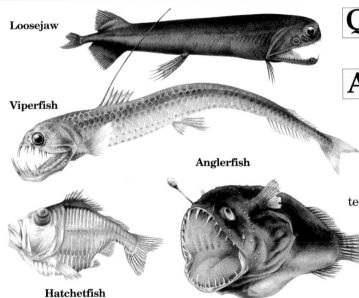

Q What lives at the bottom of the sea?

A It is very dark in the deep sea but many strange fish and other creatures live there. The loosejaw has a huge gaping mouth which traps food. The viperfish is a fierce predator with long, sharp teeth. The hatchetfish has bulging eyes which help it see clearly in the gloom. The anglerfish attracts its prey by waving a shining lure on its snout.

Q Do all fish lay eggs?

A No. Several species, such as the sailfin molly (below), keep their eggs inside until they hatch. Then they give birth to as many as 200 live young.

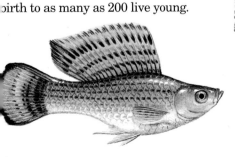

Q How do cod find their food?

A Some species of fish, such as the Atlantic cod (below) have a single whisker-like projection on their chins to help them feel for their food. This is called a barbel.

AMPHIBIANS & REPTILES

Q Are all snakes poisonous?

A Many snakes are perfectly harmless to humans and do not have poison fangs or venom. Although it may look menacing, this Arafura wart snake (above), which lives in rivers in Australia and New Guinea, does not have a poisonous bite.

Q What is a salamander?

A Salamanders such as this tiger salamander (right) are related to newts, and both are amphibians. Salamanders are perfectly at home on land but have to live in damp places. This is because their skins easily lose water. Some species can breed on land but many return to water to spawn. Salamanders eat small creatures such as worms and slugs.

Q How do frogs breathe?

A Like other amphibians, frogs have lungs which they use to take in air and absorb oxygen into their blood. They are also able to take up oxygen through their skins. In order to do this, however, they have to keep their bodies moist at all times. Frogs are also able to absorb oxygen through the moist lining of their mouths.

Q Which turtle travels furthest?

A Most turtles travel long distances during their lives. The green turtle (left), however, probably holds the record. Individuals that feed off the coast of South America travel 2,200 kilometres to Ascension Island to breed. Turtles make these long-distance journeys because the number of beaches suitable for egg-laying is small.

Q How does the collared lizard escape?

A The collared lizard (right) lives on grassy plains in North America. In order to escape from danger, the lizard is able to run on its back legs. It is able, therefore, to move at faster speeds than if it were having to scurry on all four legs.

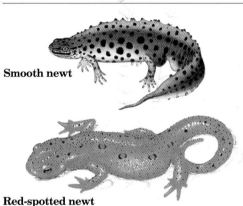

Smooth newt

Red-spotted newt

Q How do newts find their way home?

A Newts such as the smooth newt and the red-spotted newt spend much of their lives on land but return to water to breed. They often find the pond where they themselves were spawned. Most species use taste and smell to help them navigate. A few species also use the Sun or the Earth's magnetism to check the direction they are travelling in.

Q Which reptiles can change colour?

A Chameleons (left) are able to change their colour to match their background. They do this by moving pigment around in their skins, and the change can be complete in just a few minutes. Chameleons use this ability to change colour for camouflage. This way they can avoid being spotted by predators. They can also get closer to prey without being seen.

AMPHIBIANS & REPTILES

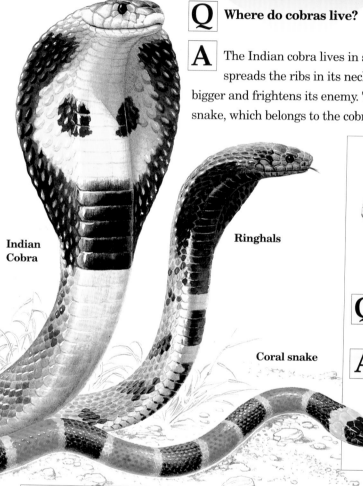

Indian Cobra

Ringhals

Coral snake

Q Where do cobras live?

A The Indian cobra lives in southern Asia. When threatened, it spreads the ribs in its neck, forming a hood. This makes it appear bigger and frightens its enemy. The ringhals is an African cobra. The coral snake, which belongs to the cobra family, lives in the American forests.

Q How can a chameleon look in two places at once?

A A chameleon can swivel its eyes separately. One may be looking forwards, and the other backwards. The eyes can also work together to focus on the same object.

Alligator

Crocodile

Q How can you tell the difference between an alligator and a crocodile?

A When a crocodile closes its mouth, the fourth tooth in the lower jaw sticks up outside the top jaw. When an alligator does the same thing, this tooth is hidden.

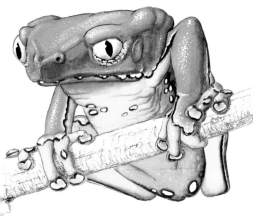

How do frogs climb trees?

A The tree frog (left) has round discs at the end of its toes. These act as suckers and help the frog to climb up smooth leaves. The toes are long and can curl round thin twigs. Some tree frogs have sticky webbing between their fingers and toes which enable them to hold on more easily. The frog's belly skin is loose and this also clings to the tree.

Q **Why do reptiles flick out their tongues?**

A This monitor lizard (right) is flicking out its tongue. Sometimes the tongue touches the ground, and sometimes it waves in the air. The tongue collects tiny chemical traces and takes them back to the mouth where nerve cells work out what the chemicals mean. By doing this, the monitor can pick up signals about food dangers nearby. Many lizards and snakes use their tongues in the same way.

Q **How do frogs jump?**

A A frog hops and leaps in just the same way as it swims. It lifts its front legs off the ground and pushes off with its powerful back legs (left). The pressure forces open the large webbed feet, giving the frog a firm base from which to jump. It lands on its front legs and chest and then gathers in its back legs, ready for another leap.

BIRDS

Q Why are birds' beaks different?

A Each bird species has a beak whose shape is best suited to the way it feeds. Birds of prey (1) have hooked beaks for tearing flesh, while waders (2) have long beaks for probing the mud for worms. Kookaburras (3) have stabbing beaks for catching reptiles, while nightjars (4) have wide gapes to catch flying insects. Puffins (5) use their beaks both for catching food and to send signals.

Q Why do vultures have bald heads?

A Vultures (right) feed on the carcasses of dead animals. They sometimes have to push their heads inside the body in order to get a meal. If they had feathers on their heads and necks, these would soon become clogged and matted with blood.

Q Which bird is the pirate of the air?

A Frigatebirds are large seabirds that live in the tropics. Instead of catching their own food, they behave like pirates towards other birds. When a frigatebird sees a bird such as a booby returning from a fishing trip, it gives chase. It pulls the victim's tail and wings until it drops its food. The frigatebird then catches the fish in mid-air.

Booby

Frigatebird

Q What is a cockatoo?

A Cockatoos are types of parrot. They can raise their head feathers to form a crest. Most species come from Australia and New Guinea. The palm cockatoo is the largest cockatoo and also the largest Australian parrot. It lives in rainforests. The galah is sometimes called the roseate cockatoo and also comes from Australia. It is the commonest cockatoo and lives near farmland.

Galah

Palm cockatoo

Q How many feathers does a bird have?

A The number of feathers on a bird varies according to the species, its age and the season. Most small songbirds have between 1,500 and 3,000 feathers on their bodies. A swan, however, might have as many as 25,000 feathers. A bird of prey, such as this eagle (left), would have between 5–8,000 feathers.

Q How does a woodpecker find its food?

A Woodpeckers (below) have large, chisel-like bills and a strong skull. When they tap the trunk of a tree, they can tell if an insect grub is living inside by the sound the tapping makes. When they find a likely spot, they smash open the wood with heavy blows from the bill. They can then take the insect to eat.

Q How did the secretary bird get its name?

A Secretary birds (right) have strange-looking feathers arranged on their heads. When the first explorers visited Africa and saw these birds they reminded them of Victorian secretaries who used to keep their quill pens behind their ears. Secretary birds catch snakes with their long legs.

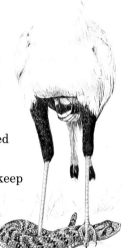

BIRDS

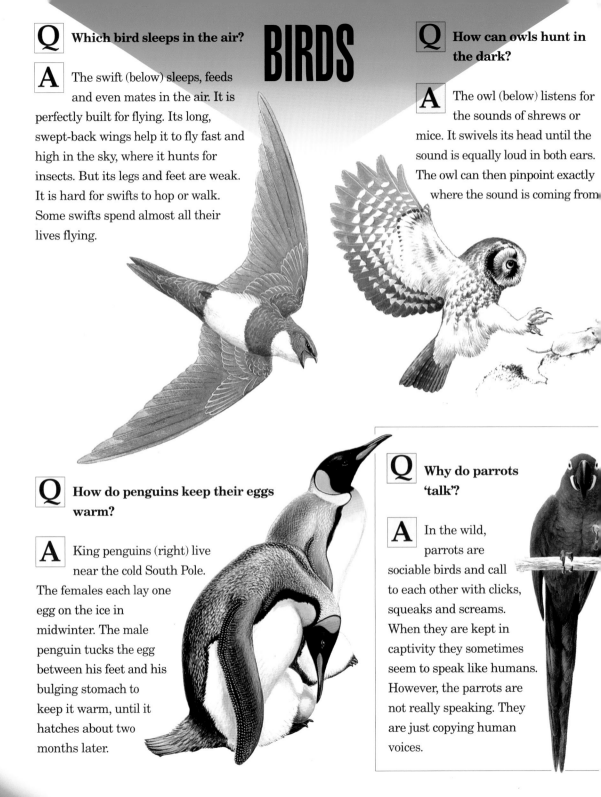

Q Which bird sleeps in the air?

A The swift (below) sleeps, feeds and even mates in the air. It is perfectly built for flying. Its long, swept-back wings help it to fly fast and high in the sky, where it hunts for insects. But its legs and feet are weak. It is hard for swifts to hop or walk. Some swifts spend almost all their lives flying.

Q How can owls hunt in the dark?

A The owl (below) listens for the sounds of shrews or mice. It swivels its head until the sound is equally loud in both ears. The owl can then pinpoint exactly where the sound is coming from.

Q How do penguins keep their eggs warm?

A King penguins (right) live near the cold South Pole. The females each lay one egg on the ice in midwinter. The male penguin tucks the egg between his feet and his bulging stomach to keep it warm, until it hatches about two months later.

Q Why do parrots 'talk'?

A In the wild, parrots are sociable birds and call to each other with clicks, squeaks and screams. When they are kept in captivity they sometimes seem to speak like humans. However, the parrots are not really speaking. They are just copying human voices.

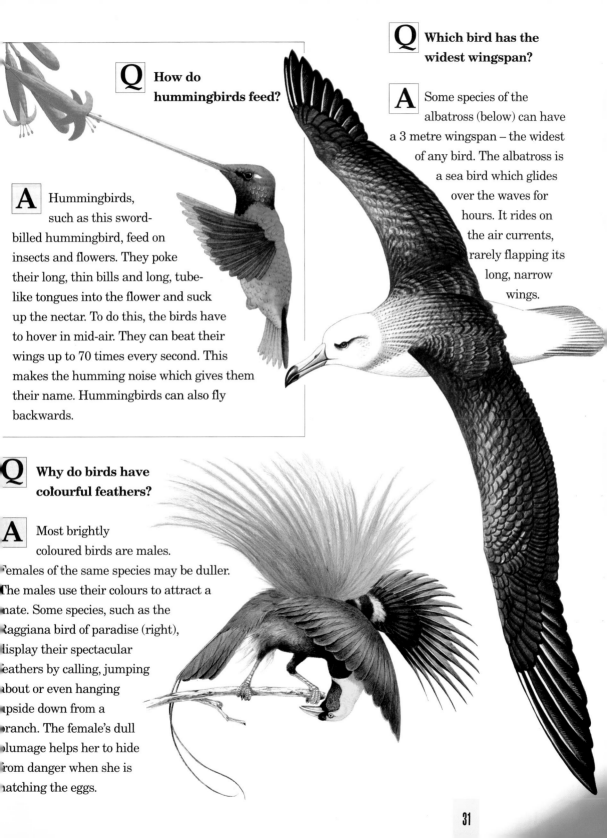

Q How do hummingbirds feed?

A Hummingbirds, such as this sword-billed hummingbird, feed on insects and flowers. They poke their long, thin bills and long, tube-like tongues into the flower and suck up the nectar. To do this, the birds have to hover in mid-air. They can beat their wings up to 70 times every second. This makes the humming noise which gives them their name. Hummingbirds can also fly backwards.

Q Which bird has the widest wingspan?

A Some species of the albatross (below) can have a 3 metre wingspan – the widest of any bird. The albatross is a sea bird which glides over the waves for hours. It rides on the air currents, rarely flapping its long, narrow wings.

Q Why do birds have colourful feathers?

A Most brightly coloured birds are males. Females of the same species may be duller. The males use their colours to attract a mate. Some species, such as the Raggiana bird of paradise (right), display their spectacular feathers by calling, jumping about or even hanging upside down from a branch. The female's dull plumage helps her to hide from danger when she is hatching the eggs.

SEA MAMMALS

Q What is the largest animal in the world?

A The blue whale (below) is the largest animal that has ever lived on this planet. It can grow to 27 metres long, and weigh 190 tonnes.

Q Can polar bears swim?

A Polar bears (above) are strong swimmers, and can travel long distances in the icy waters of the Arctic. Their fur is thick and waterproof, and their feet are partly webbed.

Q Which whale can dive the deepest?

A The sperm whale (right) can dive to a depth of more than 3,000 metres. It goes down to the seabed in search of squid to eat. Sperm whales can spend over an hour under water before coming to the surface to breathe.

Q What is a dugong?

A A dugong, or sea cow, is a mammal which lives in the warm waters of the Southwest Pacific. It eats sea grasses which it digs up from the shallows. It is a good swimmer, with a flat, forked tail.

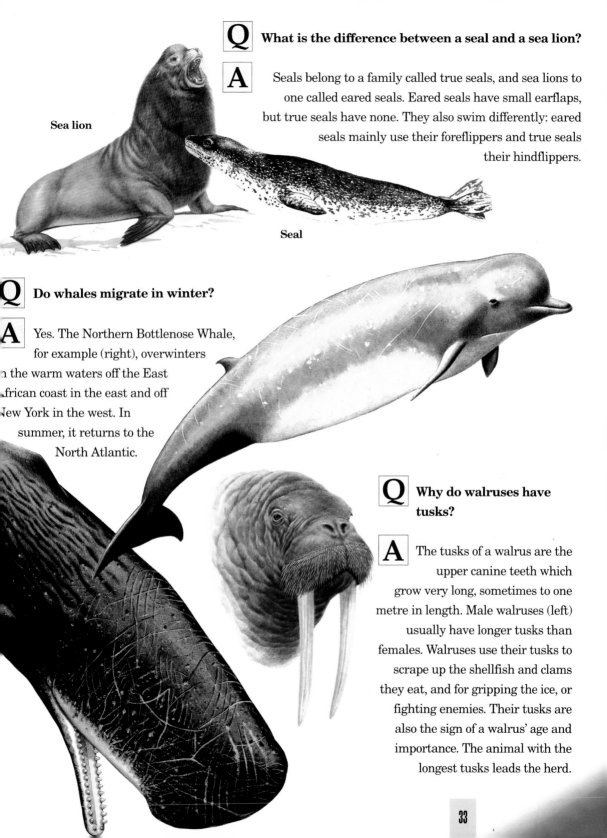

Q What is the difference between a seal and a sea lion?

A Seals belong to a family called true seals, and sea lions to one called eared seals. Eared seals have small earflaps, but true seals have none. They also swim differently: eared seals mainly use their foreflippers and true seals their hindflippers.

Sea lion

Seal

Q Do whales migrate in winter?

A Yes. The Northern Bottlenose Whale, for example (right), overwinters in the warm waters off the East African coast in the east and off New York in the west. In summer, it returns to the North Atlantic.

Q Why do walruses have tusks?

A The tusks of a walrus are the upper canine teeth which grow very long, sometimes to one metre in length. Male walruses (left) usually have longer tusks than females. Walruses use their tusks to scrape up the shellfish and clams they eat, and for gripping the ice, or fighting enemies. Their tusks are also the sign of a walrus' age and importance. The animal with the longest tusks leads the herd.

SEA MAMMALS

Bottle-nosed dolphin

Common porpoise

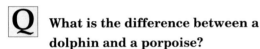

Q **Which animal is called the sea canary?**

A The beluga whale (above), which lives in arctic seas, is called the sea canary. This is because it makes a wide variety of clicking and chirping noises and sometimes snaps its jaws together as well. In the summer, belugas move into the mouths of rivers to feed on migrating salmon. They sometimes gather in large numbers to feed, and their canary-like sounds can be heard from above the water as well as from below. Adult belugas are white but their young are darker in colour.

Q **What is the difference between a dolphin and a porpoise?**

A A dolphin is larger than a porpoise (above) and has a beak-nose; it also has a large hump on its forehead. The porpoise is the smallest of the whales and does not have the dolphin's 'beak'. Instead it has a rather stubby, rounded head. Dolphins and porpoises are both types of small whale. They feed on fish and can swim very fast to catch their prey.

Q **How did the right whale get its name?**

A Sad though it may seem, early whalers gave the right whale its name. They considered it to be the 'right' whale to catch because it was a slow swimmer and floated after it had been killed. Some species of whale sink after they have been killed and would have been difficult for early whalers to tow back to their ship. Right whales were nearly hunted to extinction.

Q Which is the most ferocious sea mammal?

A The killer whale (below) is the most ferocious sea mammal. It eats fish, squid, sharks and even seals, porpoises and walruses. Sometimes killer whales launch themselves from the sea to snatch seals from the beach. Packs of killer whales have even been known to attack animals as large as blue whales. Surprisingly, attacks on humans have never been known, and killer whales can be watched closely from boats.

Q How does the sea otter eat clams?

A The sea otter lives in the north Pacific waters off California, USA. It has developed a clever method of opening clams and mussel shells to reach the food inside. Lying on its back on the surface of the sea, the sea otter places a large stone on its chest. It then strikes the clam or mussel shell against the stone until the shell shatters. The sea otter can then easily reach the food inside the shell.

LAND MAMMALS

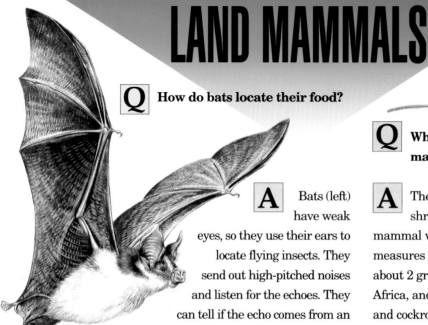

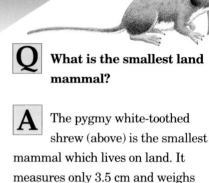

Q How do bats locate their food?

A Bats (left) have weak eyes, so they use their ears to locate flying insects. They send out high-pitched noises and listen for the echoes. They can tell if the echo comes from an insect, and work out exactly where it is.

Q What is the smallest land mammal?

A The pygmy white-toothed shrew (above) is the smallest mammal which lives on land. It measures only 3.5 cm and weighs about 2 grams. Pygmy shrews live in Africa, and eat spiders, grasshoppers and cockroaches – which may be almost as big as they are.

African elephant   Asian elephant

Q What is the difference between the African and Asian elephant?

A The African elephant is bigger than the Asian, and has larger ears. It also has two lips at the tip of its trunk instead of one.

Q Which is the fastest mammal?

A The cheetah (right) can sprint in short bursts at a speed of nearly 100 kph, faster than any other land animal. It stalks its prey until it is very close, then breaks cover and runs in long, fast strides.

Q How does a camel survive in the desert?

A Camels (right) can go for weeks without drinking. They lose very little water from their sweat or urine. The camel's fur coat protects it from the heat of the Sun, and it can close its nostrils to keep out sand and dust. Wide feet help it to walk over soft sand without sinking. Despite popular belief, camels do not store water in their humps. The humps are used to store fat, which is used for food.

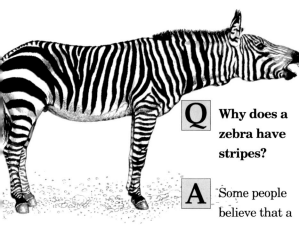

Q Why does a zebra have stripes?

A Some people believe that a zebra's stripes (above) act as a sort of camouflage, making individual animals hard to spot. But now scientists think there are other reasons for the stripes. They may dazzle lions and other cats which attack the zebra. Or they may help the members of a zebra herd to recognize each other.

Q How can you tell a monkey from an ape?

A Monkeys and apes are both primates. Apes, such as the gorilla, have no tails. They have strong arms which are longer than their legs. Most monkeys, like the woolly monkey, have tails with which they can hang from trees.

Woolly Monkey

Gorilla

LAND MAMMALS

Q Which animal is called the 'walking pine cone'?

A This name is used to describe the pangolin (left). It is also sometimes called the scaly anteater. Most of the pangolin's body is covered in hard, protective, overlapping scales. When threatened, it curls into a ball. Some pangolins can climb trees.

Q Which animal is called the riverhorse?

A The hippopotamus (above) is sometimes called the riverhorse. In fact its name is made up of Greek and Latin words meaning 'river' and 'horse'. Hippos live in Africa and spend much of the day partly under the water in rivers and lakes. After dark, they may come out to feed on the plants on the bank. Hippos can be quarrelsome animals and two males will often fight one another sometimes causing injuries.

Q What is a rhino's horn made from?

A Although it may look solid and bony, the horn of a rhino (below) has a hollow centre and is made from the same material as hair and hooves. Rhinos are sometimes illegally killed for their horns, in the belief that the horn makes a good medicine. As a result, rhinos are rare and endangered today even though the trade in their horns is banned in most countries.

Q How does a mongoose defeat a cobra?

A The deadly cobra is usually no match for a mongoose. The mongoose is extremely agile, and leaps away when the snake tries to strike. Soon the snake tires, and then the mongoose attacks, killing the snake with a bite to the neck.

Q **How does a lion catch its prey?**

A Although its prey may be fast-moving, a lion is stealthy and will creep close to its victim before making its attack. Lions often work as a team with different individuals cutting off the prey's line of escape. Animals such as this wildebeest (right) are sometimes killed with a bite to the neck which crushes the vertebrae. On other occasions, the lion suffocates its prey by gripping on to the throat.

Q **How do kangaroos and wallabies run?**

A Kangaroos and wallabies run using their large and powerful back legs to hop. The small front legs are used only for feeding and grooming. The long, robust tail helps the animal balance when it is hopping. Some kangaroos can reach speeds of 40 km/h or more and are able to hop for long periods of time. Kangaroos live in Australia.

Q **How does the porcupine protect itself?**

A The sharp, spiny quills of a porcupine are really just specially strengthened hairs. In some species, such as the African porcupine (left), they can reach a length of 50 centimetres. The quills are so strong that they can cause painful injuries if they are jabbed into a would-be attacker.

ANIMAL BEHAVIOUR

Q How do musk ox protect their young?

A When threatened by enemies, such as wolves, a herd of musk ox (right) form a line facing them, or form a circle with the calves in the middle (below). Big males then dash out and jab the attackers with their huge, powerful, curved horns.

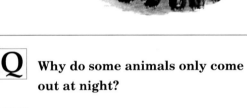

Q Why do some animals only come out at night?

A Animals that only come out at night are called nocturnal. They may be nocturnal in order to catch other nocturnal animals or to avoid daytime predators, or both. Nocturnal animals often have large eyes and good eyesight. They also need a keen sense of smell and good hearing to listen for danger.

Q How do chimps show their moods?

A Scientists have shown that chimps (left) show their moods through their facial expressions. The shape of the mouth, and whether or not the teeth are bared, are important signals. From top to bottom, the chimps are showing a desire to play, begging for food, intense fear and, lastly, anxiety.

Q How does the honeyguide get its name?

A Honeyguides (below) come from Africa and are so-called because they lead honey badgers and humans to the nests of wild bees using a series of calls. After the nest has been raided for honey, the honeyguide gets the chance to feed on bee grubs from the open nest.

Q How are young cuckoos reared?

A Female cuckoos (below) lay their eggs in the nests of other birds and then abandon their offspring. The host bird has the task of feeding and rearing the young cuckoo. As it grows up, the young cuckoo tips the host bird's eggs and young from the nest. By the time it is ready to leave the nest, the young cuckoo may be several times the size of its long-suffering foster parent.

Q Why do animals defend their territory?

A Not all animals have territories but many do. If food is limited, the animal may defend a territory to guard its food supply. With other species, such as these cassowaries (right), the males fight over a territory in which to nest and rear their young. Territorial animals know exactly where the boundaries of their own territory lie.

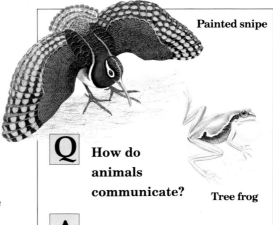

Painted snipe

Tree frog

Q How do animals communicate?

A Animals signal to each other mainly by using visual signals, such as shape or colour, and by sound. Birds such as the painted snipe have showy wings which they fan out to make an impression. Many birds sing to mark their territories or attract a mate. Most frogs produce a croaking song to mark their territories or attract a mate.

FARM ANIMALS

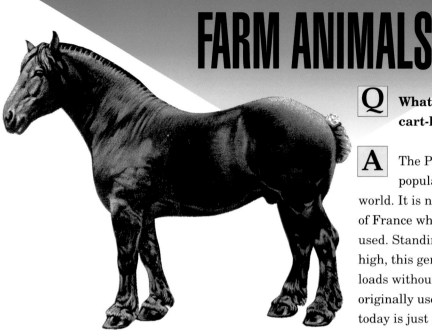

Q What is the most popular cart-horse?

A The Percheron (left) is the most popular cart-horse breed in the world. It is named after Perche, the regio of France where it was first developed an used. Standing more than 16.1 hands high, this gentle giant can pull immense loads without much effort. It was originally used for pulling heavy loads bu today is just as popular as a show horse.

Q How are beef and dairy cattle different?

A Dairy cattle, such as this Friesian and Dairy Shorthorn, are lighter in build than beef cattle. The udders are big so that they can hold large volumes of milk. Before a dairy cow can produce milk, she has to give birth to a calf. After the birth, she continues to produce milk for up to 10 months or so. Dairy cows are usually milked twice a day.

Berkshire

Duroc

Tamworth

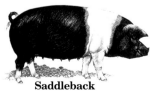

Saddleback

Q What meats do pigs provide?

A Pigs are reared for their meat which is either eaten fresh as pork, or in cured form as bacon and ham. Different pig breeds serve different needs. The Duroc, Berkshire and Saddleback are pork breeds while the Tamworth is a bacon breed.

Q Why are there different cattle breeds?

Santa Gertrudis

A Different breeds of cattle are suited to different climates around the world. The most successful breed of beef cattle is the Hereford. It is ideal for cool climates. For hot climates, breeds such as the Kankrej are ideal. It is popular in India. The Santa Gertrudis also thrives in hot places and is widely farmed in Texas, USA.

Kankrej

Hereford

Q Why do people raise chickens?

A People keep chickens (right) for three main reasons: for their meat, for their eggs and lastly for show. There are many different breeds. The Leghorn is the best egg-laying breed while the Barnvelder is kept for meat.

Leghorn **Barnvelder**

Q What is sheep wool used for?

A The quality of sheep wool varies from breed to breed and can be used for a range of purposes. The wool from the German Blackface is fine and makes excellent cloth. That from the Corriedale is coarse and springy and is used for tweeds and carpets.

Corriedale

Q How long have people kept goats?

A Goats (right) have been kept as herd animals for at least 9,000 years. They are bred for a variety of purposes. Their meat and skins are both useful and in some countries goats are used to carry loads. In many countries, goat numbers are very high and they damage wild plant life by overgrazing.

German Blackface

PETS

Q Who were the first people to keep cats as pets?

A The first people to keep cats (right) were probably the ancient Egyptians, over 3,000 years ago. Cats caught the mice, rats and other vermin which raided the grain stores. The cats were well looked after and became pets. In the end, they were worshipped as part of the Egyptian religion. Anyone who killed a cat would be sentenced to death. Some dead cats were even turned into mummies.

Q Why do some rabbits have lop ears?

A This brown and grey lop rabbit has very long, drooping ears. Lops have been specially bred over several centuries by mating does (female rabbits) and bucks (male rabbits) with long ears. Other rabbits (such as chinchillas) are bred to have long fur.

Q Which is the biggest scent hound in the world?

A The biggest of the scent hounds is the bloodhound (right). It has an extremely good sense of smell, more than a million times better than a human's, and is used to track criminals. Hounds are often bred with particular characteristics to help them hunt their prey. Otterhounds, for example, are excellent swimmers and beagles are bred for stamina, enabling them to run long distances.

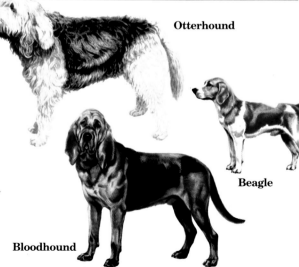

Otterhound

Beagle

Bloodhound

Q How quickly do mice breed?

A A female mouse is ready to have babies when she is seven weeks old. Three weeks after this, she could give birth to as many as ten young. She may go on producing new litters of babies every 20 to 30 days. In one year, a single mouse could have more than 100 babies!

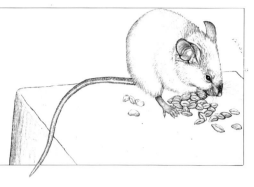

Shubunkin   **Common goldfish**

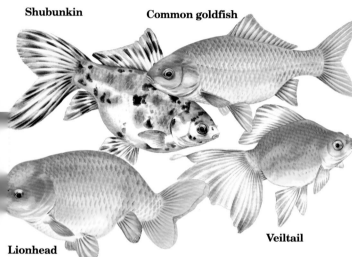

Lionhead

Veiltail

Q How did budgerigars get their name?

A Budgerigars (below) derived their name from the Australian Aboriginals. The Aboriginals like to catch and eat this wild bird so they call it 'betcherrygah', which means 'good cockatoo'. Budgerigars are popular as cage birds. They are brightly coloured and can be taught to mimic the human voice.

Q How many kinds of goldfish are there?

A Goldfish (above) are related to the wild carp. The Chinese have bred carp in ponds for over 2,000 years. They probably picked out the red- and gold-coloured fish and kept them as pets. There are now more than 150 different varieties of goldfish and its close relative, the koi carp. The shubunkin is covered with grey, gold, red or blue patches, with black markings. The common goldfish is very hardy and can live through very cold winters, even if the water ices over. Some goldfish have been bred to have special features. The lionhead has a swelling on top of its head. The veiltail has a long double tail which hangs down like a veil. Other varieties have bubbles on either side of the head, or scales which are almost invisible.

INDEX